Animals of the World

Bengal Tiger

By Edana Eckart

Children's Press®
A Division of Scholastic Inc.
New York / Toronto / London / Auckland / Sydney
Mexico City / New Delhi / Hong Kong
Danbury, Connecticut

Photo Credits: Cover and p. 5 © John Conrad/Corbis; pp. 7, 15 © Renee Lynn/Corbis; p. 9 © Terry Whittaker; Frank Lane Picture Agency/Corbis; p. 11 © Charles Philip/Corbis; p. 13 © Chase Swift/Corbis; p. 17 © Tom Brakefield/Corbis; p. 19 © Ruth Cole/Animals Animals; p. 21 © Mc Donald Wildlife Photography/Animals Animals
Contributing Editor: Jennifer Silate
Book Design: Mindy Liu

Library of Congress Cataloging-in-Publication Data

Eckart, Edana.
   Bengal tiger / by Edana Eckart.
   v. cm. — (Animals of the world)
   Contents: Bengal tigers — Cubs — Hunting.
   ISBN 0-516-24294-6 (lib. bdg.) — ISBN 0-516-27881-9 (pbk.)
   1. Tigers—Juvenile literature. [1. Tigers.] I. Title.

QL737.C23E34 2003
599.756—dc21

                                        2002154957

Contents

The **Bengal tiger** lives in **forests** in **Asia**.

5

Most Bengal tigers are orange and white.

Some are only white.

Most Bengal tigers have black **stripes**.

Bengal tiger babies are called **cubs**.

The Bengal tiger mother takes care of her cubs.

9

Bengal tigers sleep a lot during the day.

They **hunt** for food at night.

11

Bengal tigers can run fast.

Bengal tigers can also **swim**.

They like the water.

Bengal tigers have big eyes.

They can see very well.

Bengal tigers **roar** to talk to other animals and tigers.

Their roars can be heard from very far away.

Bengal tigers are very beautiful and powerful animals.

New Words

Asia (**ay**-zhuh) the largest area of land on Earth

Bengal tiger (**ben**-guhl **tie**-guhr) a large wild cat
with orange and white fur with dark stripes

cubs (**kuhbz**) young tigers

forests (**for**-ists) large areas where many trees and
other plants grow close together

hunt (**huhnt**) to search for other animals for food

roar (**ror**) to make a loud, deep noise

stripes (**stripes**) lines of color that are next to
different colors

swim (**swim**) to move forward or backward in the
water by using your arms and legs

To Find Out More

Books
Bengal Tiger
by Rod Theodorou
Heinemann Library

Bengal Tigers
by Christy Steele
Raintree/Steck Vaughn

Web Site
5 Tigers: Kids
http://www.5tigers.org
Find information about tigers, play games, and more
on this Web site.

Index

About the Author

Edana Eckart has written several children's books. She enjoys bike riding with her family.

Reading Consultants

Kris Flynn, Coordinator, Small School District Literacy, The San Diego County Office of Education

Shelly Forys, Certified Reading Recovery Specialist, W.J. Zahnow Elementary School, Waterloo, IL

Sue McAdams, Former President of the North Texas Reading Council of the IRA, and Early Literacy Consultant, Dallas, TX